Your Amazing Itty Bitty™ Magic Mind Book

15 Secrets to Wellness and Success Using the Science of Your Mind

Jenny Harkleroad

Published by Itty Bitty™ Publishing
A subsidiary of S & P Productions, Inc.
Copyright © 2024 **Jenny Harkleroad**

All rights reserved. No part of this book may be reproduced or transmitted in any form or by any means, electronic or mechanical, including photocopying, recording, or by any information storage and retrieval system, without written permission of the publisher, except for the inclusion of brief quotations in a review.

Printed in the United States of America

Itty Bitty Publishing
311 Main Street, Suite D
El Segundo, CA 90245
(310) 640-8885

ISBN: 978-1-7322946-8-4

*Disclaimer, I am not a doctor, psychologist, scientist, or medical specialist. Always consult a professional when you have medical concerns.

Your Amazing Itty Bitty™ Magic Mind Book

15 Secrets to Wellness and Success Using the Science of Your Mind

Are you ready to overcome problems, achieve big goals, experience personal growth, and feel great from the inside out? You don't need to be stressed out, burned out, overwhelmed or frustrated. You can turn everything around with the power of your mind.

Train your brain to leave unhappiness, worry, fear, sickness, and discomfort behind. Let go of difficult childhood experiences, pain, and regrets.

It's time to embrace a new way of being and shape the future you want to create.

In this book you will learn to:

- Clarify your goals in present tense format
- Muscle test to get answers from your body
- Train your brain for wellness and success
- Take action to solve your problems and achieve your goals

If you are ready to become who you always wanted to be, the secret is right between your ears. Pick up a copy of this powerful must-read Itty Bitty™ book today!

Dedication

To my husband, children, and parents. Thank you for loving me before I learned how to be my best self. To Warren Jacobs, M.D., who taught me about the power of my mind and helped me heal my body and my life. To my best friend Kelli for caring about me deeply and listening to my endless stories. And, to God for helping me find a solution to all my problems.

Stop by our Itty Bitty™ website to find interesting blog entries regarding Magic Mind.

www.IttyBittyPublishing.com

and

Visit Jenny Harkleroad at:

https://BalancedYou.org
https://SummitTranformation.com
https://LeapTransformationMethod.com

Table of Contents

Introduction
Step 1. Your Superpower Mind
Step 2. What Do YOU Want?
Step 3. Puppy Brain
Step 4. Your Conscious Mind
Step 5. Your Subconscious/Unconscious Mind
Step 6. Your Superconscious Mind
Step 7. It's Not Too Late!
Step 8. Your Body Knows®-Muscle Testing
Step 9. Easy Decision Making
Step 10. Training Your Brain—Goals
Step 11. Training Your Brain—Brain Exercises
Step 12. Training Your Brain—Action
Step 13. Changing the Brain With the Mind®-the Science
Step 14. Daily Practice
Step 15. Your Superpower Life

Introduction

Ready to solve problems, achieve big goals, feel different from the inside out, and grow like never before?

Let's do this!

Unhappy, unfulfilled, in pain?

You don't have to be.

Stressed out, burned out, frustrated?

Turn it around.

Worried, fearful, sick and tired?

Let's make it a thing of the past.

Hard childhood, rough past, addictions?

Learn how to let them go.

Maybe you've tried everything to solve your problems, and nothing has worked.

You've come to the right place!

Have HUGE dreams and you're not sure how to achieve them?

You are about to learn how to have, be, and do it all with *Your Magic Mind!*

Step 1
Your Superpower Mind

You are the narrator of your life story. Do you like the narration? Do you like your reality?

When you plant an apple seed, you get an apple tree. Your thoughts are seeds that bring a harvest. What seeds are you planting? Not sure? Look at your harvest.

1. Your harvest, or your life, was created through your thinking, which comes from your belief system.
2. To create a new life, you have to think differently by creating a new belief system.

Have you ever tried to lose weight and then gained it back? You were able to overpower your belief system temporarily until you lost focus and then your mind took you back to the belief system you were hoping to get past.

1. When you overpower your mind without changing your belief system, success is only temporary.
2. Your belief system is based on what you've experienced, especially early in your life.

Mindset Is a Buzzword but Something Big Is Missing!

What's missing from most mindset training is an understanding of the brain, the mind, and how they work. Also missing are the tools to change your brain using your mind.

- In this book, you'll go way beyond positive affirmations, positive thinking, and faking it until you make it.
- You become the person you've always wanted to be by changing your belief system.

You might have already heard that:

- You are creating your reality from the inside out.
- What you think about is what you bring about, and what you focus on expands.
- Your mind is the most powerful tool you'll ever own.

But how? How do you tap into that superpower mind to create health, wealth, happiness, and wonderful soulful relationships?

Thanks to modern-day science, you can now access your superpower mind and change anything you want. And you don't even need a scalpel.

Step 2
What Do YOU Want?

In order to train your brain for success, you have to know what you want. Oprah says the one thing most successful people in the world have in common is they know what they want.

1. Would you like to be more successful?
2. If your answer is yes, it's time to answer the following questions.
3. If you had a magic wand right now, what would you wish for? What do you want different in your life?
4. You will need your answer when you get to Step 10, so please write down what you want now.

It's best to have goals in all areas of life. Living a balanced life brings joy, peace, love, and health. Living an unbalanced life brings frustration and pain. Let's create your balanced life goals now.

1. What are your money goals?
2. What are your health goals?
3. What are your relationship goals?
4. What are your wellness goals?
5. What are your spiritual goals?
6. What are your professional goals?
7. What are your recreational goals?

Beyond Goals, What Is Your Purpose Or Calling?

What brings joy to your heart? Or, what makes you crazy that you need to find a solution for? Both questions can get you closer to understanding your purpose or calling.

A mentor of mine, Sandra Yancey, says, "People give up on their dreams all the time. A calling is different. You can't give up on it, because it will never give up on you."

- If you don't know your purpose or calling, think of your natural skills and abilities. What are they?
- What do people say you are great at?
- What did you want to be or do when you were young?
- If you knew your purpose or calling, what would you say it is?

Make every day count by discovering and living your purpose.

- Whether you know your purpose or not, take action.
- It's okay to change course when you gain more clarity.
- All action leads to learning, experience, and growth to help you live your purpose. Don't wait; act now.

Step 3
Puppy Brain

Have you ever had a puppy that pees on the floor, chews the couch, barks, bites, and steals your shoes? Bad puppy! That puppy needs training.

Do you have "puppy brain?" What does "puppy brain" feel like? Fear, worry, stress, pain, forgetfulness, anger, sadness, frustration, burnout, anxiousness, unhappiness, and more.

1. When your brain is trained it behaves, creating feelings of peace, balance, joy, happiness, and health.
2. When your brain is not trained, you can get distracted, forgetful, jealous, short-tempered, mad, judgmental, sick, and more.

Psychologists say you have 50,000-80,000 thoughts per day, 80% negative and 90% a repeat of yesterday. No wonder your brain keeps misbehaving. In this book, you will learn how to train your brain.

1. Decide what you want to achieve.
2. Train your brain to support your goals through brain exercises.
3. Once you know your goals, manifest them with positive action steps.

How Do You Train Your Brain?

It all starts with the 17-second rule taught to me by Dr. Jeffery Fannin, PhD, the neuroscientist who conducted brain studies on the transformation work I created. He taught the following:

- A thought is an electrical signal in your brain lasting 17 seconds. That's all it is.
- If the thought lasts more than 17 seconds, it becomes a chemical reaction within your body, causing you to think the way you feel.
- When you think the way you feel, your brain attracts like thoughts to prove that your thoughts and feelings are true—a feedback loop.
- When this continues more than 68 seconds, your energy field changes.
- Your energy field is responsible for your vibration.
- Your vibration is responsible for what you attract and manifest in your life.

If you've heard that thoughts become things, now you know why.

- Unless you want to create the reality you think about, you must stop the thought in 17 seconds or less!
- To stop a specific thought, ask yourself how you'd rather feel, what you can do to create that new reality, then go and do it.

Step 4
Your Conscious Mind

The best way for you to change your life is to understand the science of your mind. Once you understand your mind, you will be in the driver's seat of your life!

1. Your conscious mind is your decision-making mind. Your conscious mind works all day thinking, planning, strategizing, and answering questions for you based on your perceptions.
2. Scientists say the conscious mind processes about four million bits of information per second, focusing best on one task at a time.
3. Your conscious mind jumps from subject to subject as you think about different things from the past, present, and future.

Focusing your conscious mind enhances the following:

1. Better all-around performance
2. Peace of mind and focus
3. Satisfaction in daily activities
4. A sense of well-being and ease

The Difference Between the Brain And the Mind

To better understand the brain and the mind, it helps to start with these definitions:

- The **brain** is one of the largest and most complex organs in the human body, made up of more than 100 billion nerves that communicate in trillions of connections called synapses. (webmed.com)
- The **mind** is the set of faculties including cognitive aspects such as consciousness, imagination, perception, thinking, intelligence, judgment, language, memory, and non-cognitive aspects, such as emotion and instinct. (Wikipedia)

In this book, with the brain change process you learn, you will be Changing The Brain With The Mind®.

- Think of it like this: your brain is the hardware, and your mind is the software.
- In the brain training process, you will use your mind to decide what you want to change in your life, and then you will train your brain to create your new reality.

Step 5
Your Subconscious/Unconscious Mind

Your subconscious mind, sometimes called your unconscious mind, is the mind beyond awareness. In other words, below your consciousness. You don't know what's happening in that mind.

1. Your subconscious is timeless and remembers all your life experiences.
2. Your subconscious mind was programmed by those around you when you were young (mostly ages 0-8).
3. Your subconscious mind is around one million times more powerful than your conscious mind and processes thousands of tasks at the same time, according to scientists.

Your subconscious programming, also called your belief system, is the lens through which you see the world.

1. Your subconscious mind controls how you think, feel, act, and react automatically.
2. Your subconscious programming or belief system determines how your cells process the messages from your brain.

How Your First Two Minds Work Together

Your conscious mind controls your goals, and your subconscious mind controls your reality. The subconscious always wins. You can want some-thing badly, but if your subconscious is not in support, you'll never permanently reach the goal. You might temporarily hit the goal, but then you'll backslide when you lose focus on the goal. Here are some examples:

- You fall in love and then end up in divorce court. What happened? The subconscious took over!
- You commit to stop smoking or drinking but then do it again. What happened? The subconscious took over!

Don't Blink!

A great example of how your subconscious mind overpowers your conscious mind is blinking, which is a subconscious program. You can overpower the subconscious mind with your conscious mind, but only temporarily. Try it. You can avoid blinking until your conscious mind gets distracted, and your subconscious mind takes over again. If you want to change your life easily and permanently, you must change your subconscious programming.

Step 6
Your Superconscious Mind

You've probably heard of your conscious mind and your subconscious mind, but what is your superconscious mind?

1. Your superconscious mind is a level of awareness beyond the physical.
2. The superconscious communicates in energetic vibration.
3. Scientifically, this communication happens vibrationally through the thalamus, your body's information relay system, to your cells. You also communicate vibrationally from your cells back through your thalamus.

What are other names for your superconscious mind?

1. Your higher self
2. God
3. Holy Ghost or Holy Spirit
4. Your gut instinct
5. Intuition
6. Your inner wisdom or inner knowing
7. Collective consciousness
8. The Universe
9. Your soul or spirit

The Superconscious Mind Is Typically Quiet and Subtle

The best way to tap into the superconscious mind is being quiet and still. In this busy world, you might not always give yourself the opportunity for quiet time. But when you do, a whole new world will open up for you—the world of the superconscious.

- The more you listen to your superconscious, the better you get at hearing it.
- Your superconscious is like a radio station always playing. However, you can only hear the station if you tune in.
- Why would you want to tune into this mind? Because all the secrets of the universe can be revealed to you. That is worth getting quiet for!

Here are some ways to hear, feel or experience your subconscious mind.

- Ask questions in prayer
- Meditation
- Journaling
- Reading spiritual books
- Visiting holy places
- Listen to spiritual leaders
- Reading scripture
- Spend time in nature

Step 7
It's NOT Too Late!

If your life isn't the way you want it to be, you can change it! It's never too late to tap into the infinite power of your mind.

1. Describe the life you want to live.
2. Instead of thinking about what you don't like about your life, learn to create the life of your dreams, whether physical, mental, spiritual, financial, or emotional.

Have you tried to make life changes to achieve your dreams, but you keep getting stuck, frustrated, and give up making real lasting changes? First, you are not alone! Second, you feel this way because:

1. You haven't tapped into the power of all your minds.
2. Most of your efforts are spent on your conscious mind, your least powerful mind.
3. Your belief system keeps you stuck in the same patterns of thinking and being.
4. You still need to learn how to retrain your brain.

I Want It NOW!

Have you ever felt this way? It's interesting that sometimes the harder we push, the more impossible it seems. Try the following instead.

- Surrender to time and let life unfold.
- Focus on your clarity of purpose, your calling, and work toward it.
- Never get discouraged; be believing. Believing keeps you in the vibration of attracting your desires.
- Act constructively to manifest your goals.

Before Roger Banister broke the world record of running a sub-four mile, scientists said it wasn't humanly possible. But once he did it, others knew it was possible. Now 1,700+ athletes have run a sub-four mile too. Impossible? Only if you think it is.

- You are only limited by what is between your ears.
- Stop believing limiting thoughts and start believing in the possible.
- Look for people who have done what you want; you can do it if they did it.
- If nobody has done it yet, choose to be the next Roger Banister.
- Do the seemingly impossible and lead the way.

Step 8
Your Body Knows®-Muscle Testing

You might believe that knowledge is in your brain, but it's also in your body. Your Body Knows® the answers that your brain can't tell you through thoughts. How can you know what you believe subconsciously? With a muscle test!

1. Muscle testing was discovered in 1964 by Dr. George J. Goodheart.
2. A live muscle test is most often done by pressing on a raised arm resisting downward pressure.
3. In 1999, a computerized study of muscle testing was done and published in *Perceptual and Motor Skills* finding that when something was false during a muscle test, the arm went down 58.9% faster with 17.2% less pressure.

In the Summit Transformation® brain training process a muscle test is used with private clients to determine:

1. If the client believes in their goal
2. The correct brain exercise to help the client achieve their goal
3. Confirmation that the brain exercise changed the client's subconscious belief

Remote Muscle Testing

Live muscle testing is only helpful when you are with another person. If you're alone, however, there is still a way!

- Your body is highly complex and easily reads the energy of another person, even remotely.
- You can be on the opposite side of the world, and it works immediately!
- Your body is the tool for a remote muscle test.

Instead of pressing on an arm to see if it moves when a goal is stated, touch your first finger and thumb together tightly on each hand and interlace them to make interlocking finger rings. Try to pull the rings apart when you state your goal.

- When someone states a goal they believe subconsciously and you try to pull your finger rings apart, it's harder to get them separated.
- When someone states a goal they do NOT believe subconsciously, it's easier to pull your finger rings apart.
- Practice this by testing your true and false name. The more you practice, the better you get.

Step 9
Easy Decision-Making!

One of my favorite things about muscle testing is it's the secret to making decisions. Your Body Knows® what's best for you, but your conscious mind clouds the easy decision. Achieve easy decision-making with a muscle test.

1. A muscle test is not a blood test or a scientific fact. A muscle test checks your subconscious beliefs.
2. You can trick yourself in a muscle test, so you must remain open and curious to get an accurate answer.
3. The more you practice muscle testing, the more you trust the answers you get.

A sway test is one of the easiest self-muscle tests. Anyone can do it at any time if you can stand up.

1. Tell your body that if something is true, you want it to sway forward, and if something is not true, you want it to sway backward.
2. Stand up. Say your real name and wait. Feel the forward pull. Then say your false name and wait. Feel the backward pull. It's not magic, it's the wisdom of your body following your instructions.

Next Time You Need to Decide, Just Sway!

Remind your body what to do. True or yes, you sway forward; false or no, you sway backward.

- Start with something small, like what you want for lunch. Say, "I want a sandwich for lunch." Wait and feel. Then say, "I want a salad for lunch." Wait and feel.
- Always remain open and curious. Never try to make your body respond the way you want it to. Trust that your body has the best answer for you.

As you gain expertise doing remote muscle testing, use the finger rings or the sway test to easily make decisions. Remember to stay open and curious, allowing your body to show you what's best by tapping into your higher knowing. You can use this skill to help others, too. For example:

- Your daughter calls from college. She says, "Mom, should I drop the class I'm struggling with or stick with it?"
- Say, "Let's find out what's best for you."
- Have your child say, "I should drop the class." Do a muscle test on yourself for your child or have them sway.
- Have your child say, "I should stick with the class." Do a muscle test on yourself for your child or have them sway.
- This is parenthood made simple!

Step 10
Training Your Brain—Goals

Changing your life starts with a goal. To train your brain to create the life you want, you first need to know what you want.

1. If you're still unclear about what you want, go back to Step 2 to clarify what you want to be different in your life.
2. Focus on what you want to create when writing your goals.

Once you've decided what you want, write your goal statement as a positive affirmation that already exists in your life. Here are some examples of great goal statements:

1. I am happy, healthy, and wealthy.
2. I get along great with my family, friends, and coworkers.
3. I have plenty of money saved to retire in comfort.
4. I easily fall asleep, stay asleep, and wake up refreshed.
5. My body and mind are filled with peace.
6. Lots of people love and appreciate me.
7. I feel safe in the world.
8. I easily let the past go.
9. My life is filled with fun.
10. I am grateful to be me.

Create a Balanced Mix of Specific and Broad Goals

If you want to be healthy, select a broad goal like, "I look and feel great." You can also have more specific goals like, "It's easy to make healthy food choices," and, "I enjoy exercising daily."

- Start a list of goals that improve your personal and professional life.
- Work on at least one goal each day by training your brain to believe in the goal by doing a brain exercise (Step 11), then take action to accomplish the goal (Step 12).

How do you have enough goals to keep training your brain every day? It's easier than you think!

- Keep asking yourself what you want to be different in your life, then write more goal statements.
- Remember the 17-second rule and pay attention to your thoughts.
- Negative thinking will lead to endless goal statements when you turn negative thoughts around.
- Life happens! There are always new twists and turns, ups and downs, which give you plenty of opportunities to create goal statements to work on your thinking, belief system, and reality every day.

Step 11
Training Your Brain—Brain Exercises

Henry Ford knew a lot about the power of the mind when he said, "Whether you think you can or you think you can't; either way you're right."

1. Train your brain to believe in your goals. Doing so changes your subconscious belief system and helps you accomplish your goals with one million times the power your conscious mind can offer.
2. Close your eyes during brain exercises and take slow breaths to slow your brain down to a more programmable state.

Summit Transformation® was created in four levels with 18 brain exercises used for Changing The Brain With The Mind®.

1. Level 1 brain exercises create new beliefs.
2. Level 2 brain exercises clear hidden blocks.
3. Level 3 brain exercises get rid of opposing beliefs.
4. Level 4 brain exercises help you discover what you need to understand to achieve your goals.

Ready To Try a Brain Exercise Now?

Write a positive goal statement as we discussed in Step 10.

- Close your eyes. Cross your arms and put your hands on your shoulders like you are giving yourself a hug. Repeat your goal statement silently for one minute.
- Uncross your arms and recross them so the other hand is on top. Repeat your goal silently for one more minute.
- Uncross your arms and tap your fingertips together like there is a ball between your palms. Repeat your goal silently for one more minute.
- Next, hold your fingertips together. Repeat your goal silently for one more minute.

When you're done with the brain exercise, drink water. This process causes heat in the brain, and heat causes dehydration. Please stay hydrated for best results.

- Notice changes in your life over the next week and beyond now that your brain is supporting you in your goal.
- If the goal needs more work, do more brain exercises for your goal with new goal statements.
- Download a second brain exercise here: https://BalancedYou.org/MMB.

Step 12
Training Your Brain—Action!

The most powerful part of this brain training process is the brain exercises using your positive goal. The next most powerful part is taking action!

1. Most of the problems you want to solve or goals you want to achieve require action.
2. Action is the fertilizer for brain work.
3. Action is not repeating the goal like a positive affirmation.

Action is actionable. It is doing—acting. What can you do to help you solve the problem, achieve the goal, or feel differently?

1. If the goal has to do with weight loss, the action might be to exercise five days per week or only eat one serving of food at each meal.
2. If the goal has to do with relationships, a good action is defining what you want and need in your relationship and sharing it with your partner.
3. If the goal relates to money, you might ask for a raise, learn a new skill set to get a promotion or make more sales calls.

Taking Action Toward Your Goals.

- The brain exercise is like forging a new path in the forest and the action is like walking the path, so the path remains.
- It works best if you can make the action easy so you can do it immediately, or at least get started on it that same day.

If you are doing brain exercises in the LEAP Transformation®, (an on-demand brain training portal and app), or you take Summit Transformation® training, (online courses to learn all 18 brain exercises and get certified in this work), you are probably working on more than one goal per day. When working on lots of goals each day, you can make your action plans duplicate another goal's action plan or skip the action completely.

- The more brain exercises you do per day, the less action you need to take.
- Too many action plans can feel overwhelming. Don't get overwhelmed with action plans. Focus on brain exercises.
- If you can only choose between having time to do brain exercises or having time to take action, always choose the brain exercise.
- Brain exercises change how your brain processes life. You will start to notice that you feel different, and you will see things in a new way automatically.

Step 13
Changing the Brain With the Mind®- the Science

Dr. Jeffrey Fannin, PhD was hired to do two brain studies on this work, Summit Transformation®.

1. The first study was done to see how the brain changed from immediately before to immediately after the brain exercises.
2. The second brain study was done over a 12-week period, mapping the brain of each participant before and after the 12 weeks of brain exercises.
3. The brain studies were done working live and also working remotely over Zoom.

Dr. Fannin thought Summit Transformation® would make changes in the theta brain for most of the participants.

1. Dr. Fannin found Summit Transformation® changed not only the theta brain, but every brain phase was changed, and everyone had brain changes from the work.
2. See the brain map images and read more from both studies at: https://SummitTransformation.com/Science.

How Does Changing the Brain Change a Belief?

According to Dr. Jeffrey Fannin, PhD, in a theta brain state, you can rewrite subconscious beliefs with coherence (communication) of information and amplitude (energy) to create that coherence (communication).

According to Dr. Fannin, "Jenny's process works!" Why does it work? It works because it creates the coherence and amplitude to change brain patterns, which change subconscious beliefs, which change your cellular response, which changes the printout of your life.

- We are Changing The Brain With The Mind®.
- The fastest way to change you is to change your subconscious programming.
- Think of your subconscious mind as a computer program. It runs you about 95% of the time according to scientists like Bruce Lipton, PhD.
- When you do this work daily to retrain your subconscious programming, you'll begin to feel like a whole new you.
- The more work you do on your subconscious mind with the brain exercises in this book, the more you will be able to think and feel, act and react, and create in the way you want to.

Step 14
Daily Practice

Getting your brain in shape is just like getting your body in shape. It's not a one-and-done deal. That would be too good to be true!

1. I recommend that you do at least one brain exercise per day.
2. Focus your daily brain exercise on a problem you want to solve, or on a goal you want to achieve.
3. Brain exercises take 5-15 minutes on average.

When you train your brain each day, it changes your subconscious programming. Say goodbye to self-sabotage, mind chatter, and limiting beliefs. Say hello to creating your very best life.

1. Training your brain is like sharpening an ax before you use it.
2. Yes, it does take time to sharpen the ax but then the ax works better and faster, so the time is justified.
3. Do the brain exercise in Step 11 as well as the daily brain exercise you can download in that same step for your goals.
4. You will be amazed at what you can accomplish with your new magic mind!

What Kind of Results Do People Get Using These Brain Exercises?

As of this book writing, we've tracked the results of about 1,000 clients. About half are private clients and about half are clients working through an online brain training portal and app called LEAP Transformation®.

- Our private clients report an average of 57% improvement per goal when they do one brain exercise with our facilitators.
- Our online clients report an average of 41% improvement per goal when they do one brain exercises with LEAP Transformation®.
- You can also get great results doing the two-brain exercises in Step 11.

What if you want more than 57% improvement (private sessions) or 41% improvement (online portal)? Easy! Do more than one brain exercise related to your goal.

- If you want to know more about private sessions, schedule a free consultation at https://BalancedYou.org.
- If you'd like to know more about the portal and app for brain work, go to: https://LeapTransformationMethod.com.
- If you are looking to learn all 18 brain exercises to help yourself or others, go to https://SummitTransformation.com.

Step 15
Your Superpower Life

Create your superpower life in these four easy steps:

1. Decide what you want. (Step 2)
2. Write your goal as if it already exists. (Step 10)
3. Do a brain exercise using your goal statement. (Step 11)
4. Choose an action plan and do it. (Step 12)

If you don't like something about your life, you know how to change it with the four steps above. You have the power to create the life of your dreams. Tap into that power daily!

1. Remember that getting your brain in shape is like getting your body in shape. It takes time and effort to retrain your brain to create the life you want.
2. Be kind, loving, and patient with yourself in the process.
3. Soon you will create your superpower life by doing the work daily.
4. Once you get your life the way you want it, keep your brain trained with daily brain exercises and positive thoughts for continued improvement and growth.

Reasons You Should and Should NOT Do This Brain Work

You should NOT do this brain work if:

- You are happy with every area of your life.
- You easily accomplish all your goals.
- You have no stress, worry, or fear.
- You don't want to change.
- You always feel great.
- You have no problems.
- You have plenty of time and money.
- You can't think of anything you want to be different in your life.

You **should** do this brain work if:

- You know you are meant for more.
- You want to live up to your potential.
- You know that you get in your own way, and you are tired of it.
- You have problems you have not been able to solve.
- You want to feel better every day.
- You have big goals that you want to achieve.
- You want to enjoy each day more fully.
- You want to be happy, healthy, and wealthy.
- You are ready to live your superpower life.

You've finished. Before you go …

Post/Share that you finished this book.

Please star and rate this book.

Reviews are solid gold to writers. Please take a few minutes to give us some itty bitty feedback. Thank you!

ABOUT THE AUTHOR

Jenny Harkleroad is a #1 best-selling author, speaker, and mind-change coach and teacher. She's a mother of four, which is her greatest claim to fame! Jenny is a big-hearted entrepreneur and business leader. She built a business in San Diego over 13 years producing double digits in the millions.

With the power of her mind, Jenny overcame her past of chronic pain, addictions, bad relationships, and unhappiness. She never knew how sweet life could be until she changed her mind, and that changed everything.

Jenny has a dramatic story to share about breaking her back on a mountain cliff. That event changed everything and gave her a ferocious appetite to transform lives and help others create what's missing in their lives.

Learn more about Jenny and invite her to inspire your organization to their best wellness and success at https://BalancedYou.org/Speaker.

Hear what Jenny's clients have to say about her work at https://BalancedYou.org/testimonials.

If you enjoyed this Itty Bitty® book you might also like…

- **Your Amazing Itty Bitty™ Stress Reduction Book** – Denise Thomson, CHD

- **Your Amazing Itty Bitty™ Body Life Connection Book** – Suzy Prudden and Joan Meijer Hirshland

- **Your Amazing Itty Bitty™ Purpose Book** – Gretchen Downey

Or any of the many Amazing Itty Bitty™ books available online at www.ittybittypublishing.com

www.ingramcontent.com/pod-product-compliance
Lightning Source LLC
Chambersburg PA
CBHW061306040426
42444CB00010B/2537